How Do Microchips Work?

The Tiny Technology That Powers Our Digital World

Emas Oyaks

Disclaimer

This book is intended for informational and educational purposes only. While every effort has been made to ensure the accuracy and reliability of the information provided, the author and publisher make no representations or warranties of any kind with respect to the completeness, accuracy, or suitability of the contents. The information contained herein is not intended as professional, technical, or legal advice. Readers are encouraged to conduct their own research or consult appropriate professionals before making any decisions based on the material in this book.

The author and publisher shall not be held liable or responsible for any loss, damage, or disruption caused or alleged to be caused directly or indirectly by the use or application of any content presented in this book.

All trademarks, service marks, product names, and company names mentioned are the property of their respective owners and are used for reference purposes only. Their inclusion does not imply endorsement or affiliation.

Copyright

Table Of Contents

Introduction

Picture this: you're reading this sentence on a screen—maybe on a smartphone, a tablet, or a laptop. A blink of light, a tap of your finger, and the world shifts around you. But behind that screen, beneath the sleek glass and polished metal, something extraordinary is happening. Something so small you'd need a microscope to see it—yet so powerful, it shapes nearly every second of your modern life. That "something" is the microchip.

They are silent. Invisible. Tireless. Microchips don't just make your devices work—they are the reason they exist at all. From the first time you set an alarm on your phone to the GPS guiding your car through traffic, to the moment a doctor checks your vitals in an ER—microchips are at the core of it all. They power our conversations, store our memories, drive our decisions, and even help save lives. They're in your wristwatch and your refrigerator, your bank card and your thermostat, your child's toy and the rover exploring Mars.

And yet, most people have never truly thought about them. They've become so interwoven into our lives that we barely notice them. We swipe. We tap. We talk to digital assistants. We send satellites into orbit and stream entire seasons of our favorite shows without a second thought. But under the hood of this digital magic is a story so rich, so intricate, and so astonishing that once you know it, you'll never look at your devices—or the world—the same way again.

This book is your invitation to see what most people miss.

We'll peel back the layers of silicon and metal and expose the tiny wonders pulsing at the center of your tech-filled life. You'll travel from the dusty birthplaces of early computing to the ultra-clean rooms where today's microchips are built with atomic precision. You'll meet the brilliant minds and bold ideas that made the impossible possible—and get a front-row seat to the technologies being dreamed up now that could change everything we know... again.

But this isn't just a technical manual. It's not about circuits and code in dry, lifeless terms.

It's about discovery. About unlocking the secret language of the machines we depend on, understanding how a few billion transistors arranged just right can hold your voice, your memories, your face, your music, your dreams.

You don't need a PhD to follow along. You just need curiosity—and a willingness to peek behind the curtain. What you'll find is a universe beneath your fingertips: invisible highways of electricity, logic gates performing lightning-fast calculations, and materials engineered so precisely, they rival the complexity of nature itself.

This is the story of how we've compressed the power of entire rooms into the size of a fingernail. How we've taught sand to think. How we've turned abstract mathematics into real-world miracles. It's the story of microchips—past, present, and astonishing future.

And make no mistake: this future is closer than you think. It's already reshaping how we work, how we heal, how we connect, and how we explore. In fact, you're holding a piece of it in your hands right now.

So lean in.

What you're about to read is the hidden blueprint of the digital age. It's the magic trick behind the screen. The whispering heartbeat of our time. Once you understand how microchips work, you'll start to see them everywhere—and you'll never stop marveling at how something so small can carry the weight of the world.

Are you ready?

Let's go.

Chapter 1

From Room-Sized Machines to Fingernail-Sized Marvels

In the earliest days of computing, a single machine could fill an entire room. These behemoths, with their blinking lights and humming power supplies, were built not just to process information, but to prove that it could even be done. The idea of a device small enough to sit in your pocket, yet powerful enough to hold your entire music library, navigate you across continents, or analyze genetic data in real time, would have been pure science fiction. And yet, here we are.

The story of microchips is a story of radical transformation. It's about the relentless pursuit of smaller, faster, more efficient technology. It's about the brilliant, sometimes eccentric minds who dared to see past the limitations of their era. It's also about the rise of an invisible architecture that now powers nearly everything we touch—from the toaster in your kitchen to the spacecraft orbiting the Earth. This chapter journeys back through the history of electronics to uncover how humanity moved from vacuum tubes and punched cards to silicon wafers and nanotechnology. It's a story of breakthroughs, accidents, ambition, and the shrinking of impossibility into something you can hold in the palm of your hand.

The evolution from vacuum tubes to microchips

Long before the sleek screens and seamless apps of today, computers were born in the age of vacuum tubes—bulky, fragile, glass cylinders that acted as electronic switches. The first generation of computers, built in the 1940s and 1950s, relied on thousands of these tubes to perform even the most basic calculations. Each tube consumed significant power, generated immense heat, and was prone to failure. Rooms had to be specially cooled just to house them, and any malfunction meant hours of troubleshooting. Machines like the ENIAC (Electronic Numerical Integrator and Computer) filled entire rooms, weighed tons, and could only manage calculations that today's microchips perform in a fraction of a second.

Despite their limitations, vacuum tubes represented a major leap forward from mechanical calculators. They could switch faster, process more complex tasks, and be reprogrammed with different sets of instructions. But they weren't sustainable for a future that demanded speed, efficiency, and scalability.

The turning point came with the invention of the transistor in 1947 by John Bardeen, William Shockley, and Walter Brattain at Bell Labs. Smaller, more reliable, and far more energy-efficient than vacuum tubes, the transistor marked the beginning of a new era. These tiny devices could amplify and switch electronic signals without the need for glass enclosures or massive cooling systems. Suddenly, what once required a warehouse could be condensed into a desktop unit.

But the journey didn't stop with transistors alone. As computers evolved, engineers faced a new challenge—how to wire thousands, then millions, of these components together in a reliable, cost-effective way. The answer would come in the form of the integrated circuit.

The invention of the transistor and the integrated circuit

The transistor's invention laid the foundation for what would become the semiconductor revolution. But to truly understand the magic behind today's microchips, one must look at how this initial breakthrough was refined and scaled.

By the late 1950s, as demand for smaller and more powerful computers grew, it became clear that assembling individual transistors, resistors, and capacitors on circuit boards was too inefficient and error-prone. In 1958, a Texas Instruments engineer named Jack Kilby built the first working integrated circuit. His device, carved into a single piece of germanium, contained all the components needed for a functioning oscillator. Just a year later, Robert Noyce of Fairchild Semiconductor improved upon Kilby's design by using silicon and photolithography, a method that allowed components to be patterned onto a chip like a stencil.

These advances led to the integrated circuit—a compact chip containing thousands, and eventually millions, of transistors etched onto a thin wafer of semiconductor material. These ICs (integrated circuits) reduced the size of electronic devices dramatically, making them lighter, faster, and more reliable.

As integrated circuits became more advanced, they gave rise to new categories of devices—microprocessors, memory chips, and system-on-chip designs. Suddenly, it was possible to build computing power into everything from calculators to satellites. The 1970s saw the release of the first commercially available microprocessor—the Intel 4004—which fit the computing power of an entire room into a single chip no bigger than a fingernail.

Microchips didn't just shrink computers. They made them ubiquitous. Electronics that once were confined to government labs and elite research institutions began making their way into homes, businesses, and schools. A revolution was quietly taking place—one that would soon accelerate beyond imagination.

The rise of semiconductor technology

Silicon, one of the most abundant elements on Earth, became the star material of the microelectronics age. What made it special wasn't just its availability, but its unique electrical properties. Silicon is a semiconductor, meaning it can act both as a conductor and an insulator depending on how it's treated. This dual nature made it ideal for controlling the flow of electrical signals in a precise and efficient way.

Through processes like doping—adding tiny amounts of impurities to the silicon crystal structure—engineers could control where and how electricity flowed within a chip. These manipulations allowed the creation of transistors, the basic building blocks of all digital electronics.

By the 1980s and 1990s, semiconductor fabrication had become a global industry. Fabrication plants, or "fabs," were building chips with microscopic features—lines thinner than a human hair. Innovations in materials, photolithography, and chip design pushed the boundaries of what was possible. New generations of microchips emerged every few years, each one more powerful and efficient than the last.

At the heart of this advancement was the ability to miniaturize. The smaller the transistors, the more could fit on a chip. More transistors meant more processing power, lower energy consumption, and greater functionality. This exponential improvement led to smarter phones, faster computers, and new classes of devices that were once the stuff of science fiction.

Meanwhile, entire ecosystems grew around semiconductor technology. Startups and giants alike—Apple, Intel, AMD, Qualcomm, NVIDIA—built their fortunes on chips that got better every year. From cloud computing to artificial intelligence, from wearables to electric vehicles, semiconductors were the silent enablers of progress.

The role of Moore's Law in microchip advancement

In 1965, Gordon Moore, co-founder of Intel, made a prediction that would shape the future of technology: the number of transistors on a chip would double approximately every two years, leading to a doubling of performance and a reduction in cost per transistor. This observation, later dubbed "Moore's Law," became the benchmark for innovation in the semiconductor world.

For decades, Moore's Law held true. Engineers and scientists pushed the limits of physics to keep up with its pace. Each new generation of microchip became more powerful, more compact, and more affordable. Smartphones became more intelligent, gaming consoles more immersive, and medical equipment more precise—all fueled by this rapid progression in microchip design.

The ripple effects of Moore's Law extended far beyond computing. Entire industries emerged or transformed in its wake. The data explosion of the internet age, the rise of social media, the growth of artificial intelligence—all trace their roots to the relentless march of Moore's Law. It became a self-fulfilling prophecy: the expectation of rapid progress drove investment, which in turn drove breakthroughs.

But as transistors approached atomic scales, the physical limits of silicon began to loom. New strategies—like 3D chip stacking, quantum computing, and alternative materials—are being explored to keep the spirit of Moore's Law alive, even if its original pace slows.

Yet the legacy of Moore's Law isn't just in numbers—it's in mindset. It instilled a culture of exponential thinking in technology, encouraging engineers and innovators to imagine what comes next, to think bigger even as they build smaller.

How microchips became the foundation of modern electronics

Today, microchips are not just parts of devices—they are the beating heart of modern life. They are the invisible intelligence behind everything we take for granted. They regulate the engine in your car, route your phone calls, unlock your front door, monitor your heart rate, and guide planes across the sky. They are in kitchen appliances, industrial machines, satellites, and smart city infrastructure.

The ubiquity of microchips has redefined what it means to be connected. Devices talk to each other, learn from each other, adapt in real time. The concept of the "Internet of Things"—where everyday objects are embedded with microchips and communicate over networks—is no longer futuristic. It's now.

And as artificial intelligence and machine learning become more integrated into daily life, the role of microchips grows even more critical. Specialized chips called GPUs and TPUs are optimized to handle the immense data processing required by AI systems. These chips help computers "see," "hear," and "learn," enabling self-driving cars, language translation, medical diagnosis, and more.

From entertainment to exploration, microchips are the unseen scaffolding of the 21st century. And while they may be small, their impact is monumental. Understanding how they came to be—and where they might go next—is key to understanding the world we live in and the future we're building.

Chapter 2

What Is a Microchip?

Imagine holding in the palm of your hand a small piece of silicon no larger than your thumbnail—a component so compact, it seems almost unremarkable at first glance. Yet this tiny marvel holds the power to run your smartphone, guide a rocket to the stars, manage global financial systems, and even help diagnose medical conditions in real time. Microchips, often referred to as the "brains" behind modern devices, have quietly become the invisible engines powering our interconnected lives.

To fully appreciate the role of microchips today, it's worth stepping back and realizing how their presence has become nearly ubiquitous, yet so easily overlooked. From the moment you wake up to the buzz of your smartwatch or smartphone, to the digital clock on your microwave, the GPS in your car, and the streaming platform you unwind with at night—microchips are woven into every facet of your daily routine. They work behind the scenes, tirelessly and precisely, enabling countless functions that would be impossible without them.

Despite their seemingly magical operation, microchips are not products of mysticism or luck, but rather the culmination of decades of innovation, miniaturization, and breakthroughs in materials science and electrical engineering. Their development reflects humanity's drive to make machines not just faster and smaller, but smarter and more efficient. In truth, the microchip represents more than just a technological achievement; it symbolizes the transformation of entire industries, the birth of new economies, and the redefinition of how humans live, work, and think.

Understanding microchips isn't just a pursuit for scientists or engineers—it's essential for anyone living in the 21st century. Because behind every device we trust and depend upon lies a complex web of circuits, transistors, and logic patterns that dictate how it performs. But what exactly is a microchip? How does it work? What components make it tick? And how is it different from the other buzzwords—processors, integrated circuits, and semiconductors—that often get tossed around in tech conversations?

To the casual observer, these terms might seem interchangeable, or worse, completely obscure. But grasping their distinctions is crucial to understanding how this technology has evolved, where it stands today, and where it might take us tomorrow. The journey begins with a clear definition, followed by an exploration into the structure, function, and purpose of the microchip—a journey that uncovers not just a piece of silicon, but a cornerstone of the modern digital age.

Definition and Purpose of a Microchip

At its core, a microchip is a miniature electronic circuit etched onto a small piece of semiconductor material, typically silicon. It contains millions, sometimes even billions, of microscopic components that allow it to perform logical operations and process data. The fundamental role of a microchip is to carry out a series of instructions that control the flow of electricity within an electronic device, thereby enabling it to complete a task—whether that task is running a smartphone app, managing a factory's robotics system, or guiding a self-driving car through traffic.

What sets microchips apart from earlier forms of computation, like mechanical relays or vacuum tubes, is their scale and speed. These chips can process information at incredible speeds, measured in nanoseconds, while occupying an area smaller than a postage stamp. That balance between performance and size has opened the door to innovations that would have been unthinkable just a few decades ago.

The name "microchip" itself is a shorthand for "microelectronic chip," a term that captures its primary characteristics: smallness and functionality. These chips are built using photolithography, a sophisticated process that involves printing complex patterns onto silicon wafers using ultraviolet light and chemicals.

Once complete, a microchip resembles a black square with tiny metal pins or contact points around its edges, designed to interface with the larger systems into which it's installed.

Although they're small, microchips are designed with remarkable precision and complexity. Their structures are built to perform specific tasks—some are tailored for general computation, others for memory storage, graphics processing, communication protocols, or even environmental sensing. No matter the application, the underlying purpose remains the same: to make decisions and perform calculations at blinding speed using binary logic—strings of 0s and 1s that represent electrical signals being turned on or off.

From an industrial standpoint, microchips are the heartbeat of automation and digitalization. They enable everything from smart manufacturing systems that can monitor their own performance, to digital assistants that recognize speech patterns, to financial algorithms capable of processing millions of transactions per second. Their integration into every aspect of life makes them one of the most important inventions in modern history, quietly shaping the direction of progress one byte at a time.

The Difference Between Microchips, Integrated Circuits, and Processors

In the world of technology, it's common to hear the terms microchip, integrated circuit, and processor used interchangeably. But while they're closely related and often coexist within the same device, each term has a distinct meaning and role within electronic systems. Understanding these differences helps reveal how modern devices think, act, and respond.

Let's start with the microchip, a general term that refers to a tiny piece of silicon embedded with a complex network of miniature electronic components. Microchips are often packaged in rectangular or square casings with metal pins or solder bumps that connect them to a larger circuit board. They serve many purposes—from memory storage and signal processing to controlling entire systems. Essentially, the term "microchip" is an umbrella that can encompass processors, memory chips, sensor chips, and more.

An integrated circuit (IC) is the technical heart of a microchip. It refers specifically to the set of electronic components—transistors, resistors, capacitors, and diodes—that are integrated into a single piece of semiconductor material. The term "integrated" comes from the way all these components are built together in one compact layout, unlike early electronics where each component was separate and wired individually. Every microchip contains at least one integrated circuit. In fact, the words are sometimes used synonymously, especially in engineering circles.

However, not all integrated circuits serve the same function. Some might be simple, performing a single task like amplifying a signal. Others are far more complex and specialized.

That brings us to the processor, or central processing unit (CPU), which is a specific type of integrated circuit—and a powerful one at that. The processor is the brain of a computing device. It fetches instructions from memory, decodes them, executes calculations, and then stores or displays the result. Unlike general-purpose microchips, processors are designed to handle logic, arithmetic, and control functions on a large scale and at high speeds. A typical CPU in a modern laptop or smartphone contains billions of transistors arranged to execute billions of instructions per second.

To visualize the distinction, imagine a microchip as a book. The integrated circuit is the content inside the book—the detailed story written in miniature form. The processor, then, is a specific kind of story: a thriller that actively drives a plot forward, making decisions and creating action. Other types of microchips might contain memory instead of logic, or sensors instead of instruction handlers.

There's also a fourth term that's worth mentioning: microcontroller. A microcontroller is a type of microchip that contains a processor, memory, and input/output components all on a single integrated circuit. These are commonly found in everyday devices like washing machines, remote controls, and thermostats—compact systems that don't need the full computing power of a computer, but still need to process instructions and interact with their surroundings.

Components of a Microchip: Transistors, Logic Gates, and Circuits

At first glance, a microchip might look like a flat, black square embedded on a board of tangled wires. But hidden inside is an intricately choreographed system of electrical components, each no larger than a virus, that collectively perform billions of calculations every second. These components—transistors, logic gates, and circuits—are the essential building blocks that bring microchips to life.

The transistor is the star of the show. In many ways, it is to electronics what the cell is to life. A tiny switch made from semiconductor material, usually silicon, a transistor controls the flow of electrical signals. It can either allow electricity to pass through or block it—an action that translates to binary 1s and 0s. Multiply that by billions, and you have a machine capable of encoding vast amounts of information at incredible speed. A modern chip may contain over 100 billion transistors, each turning on and off faster than the blink of an eye.

Transistors are arranged in patterns to form logic gates, the core mechanism that allows computers to make decisions. These gates follow Boolean logic, operating with binary inputs to produce a binary output. The most basic gates—AND, OR, and NOT—can be combined to perform highly complex operations. For instance, an AND gate will output a 1 only if both inputs are 1. An OR gate, on the other hand, outputs a 1 if at least one of the inputs is 1. These fundamental logic structures determine how data flows and how instructions are executed.

But these logic gates don't work in isolation. They're organized into circuits, interconnected pathways that process specific types of data or perform targeted tasks. These circuits are grouped into functional units—like memory, arithmetic processing, and input/output management—each designed for precise operations. Some circuits perform simple mathematical calculations, while others manage the timing of tasks or the flow of data from one place to another.

What's truly extraordinary is how small all of this has become. Thanks to advances in nanotechnology and semiconductor manufacturing, engineers can now fit billions of components onto a chip just a few square millimeters in size. These components are etched into the silicon using photolithography, a process that shines ultraviolet light through masks to create incredibly fine patterns—so precise that the wires connecting transistors are thinner than strands of DNA.

Despite their size, these components must be flawlessly engineered. A single misstep in the arrangement of a logic gate or the behavior of a transistor can cause an entire system to fail. That's why chip manufacturing is done in sterile, highly controlled environments, where even a speck of

How Microchips Control and Process Digital Information

Every time a smartphone wakes from sleep, a car adjusts fuel injection for better mileage, or a smart fridge detects an open door, a microchip is orchestrating that behavior in the background. Microchips don't merely respond to external inputs—they interpret, process, and act upon them with blistering speed and precision. But what happens inside a chip when digital information is being processed? The answer lies in an elegant dance between electricity and logic.

Digital information is expressed in binary form: sequences of ones and zeros that represent everything from a musical note to a live-streamed video. At the core of microchip operation is the control and manipulation of this binary data. Transistors, acting as ultra-fast switches, play the lead role here. Each transistor's state—on or off—corresponds to a binary 1 or 0. By carefully coordinating the switching of billions of these tiny devices, the chip transforms raw binary data into meaningful operations.

Logic gates built from transistors further determine how this data flows. These gates perform fundamental operations like addition, comparison, or storage based on the binary input they receive. For instance, a microchip inside a calculator might receive the input for "5 + 3", convert these numbers into binary, and route them through a network of arithmetic logic units (ALUs). The ALUs are specialized circuits built to handle such calculations, using logic gates to carry out binary addition and output the binary result for "8".

Memory units embedded within the chip, such as RAM (Random Access Memory) or cache, allow the chip to store temporary or frequently used data. When you open an app on your phone, the instructions that tell your device what to display and how to respond are loaded into memory. The processor doesn't just execute these commands in order—it anticipates the next ones, preloads data, and optimizes responses using predictive algorithms. This memory-chip interaction is crucial for speed and efficiency.

Timing is another vital element. Every action on a chip is synchronized using a clock signal—essentially a metronome that keeps all components operating in perfect harmony. This clock ticks millions or even billions of times per second, directing the microchip to execute operations in a precisely choreographed sequence. Without this steady rhythm, digital chaos would ensue, as components might act out of turn or misinterpret signals.

Another important concept in data processing is the instruction set—the unique language a chip understands. Different families of chips (like ARM or x86 architectures) use different instruction sets, but the principle is the same: a list of commands written in binary that tell the chip what to do, when, and how. Each instruction might ask the chip to fetch data from memory, perform a calculation, or send a signal to another part of the system. These instructions are interpreted by the control unit, a specialized part of the chip that directs operations like a conductor guiding an orchestra.

Modern microchips go far beyond simple tasks. Many are designed to perform parallel processing—executing multiple instructions at once across different cores or sections of the chip. A smartphone processor, for example, might simultaneously run your navigation app, stream music, manage incoming messages, and optimize battery use. Specialized chips like GPUs (graphics processing units) are even more powerful in handling large-scale, repetitive tasks, such as rendering images or training AI models.

Finally, input/output interfaces are what connect microchips to the physical world. Sensors collect data—like light, sound, motion, or temperature—and convert them into electrical signals. Microchips interpret these signals, make decisions based on programmed logic, and send output instructions. These outputs might power a display, activate a motor, or send information over a wireless connection. In a sense, microchips act as the nervous system of electronic devices, sensing, processing, and responding to the environment in real-time.

This invisible complexity underlies the everyday ease with which we interact with technology. Whether you're scrolling through social media, relying on GPS navigation, or asking a smart speaker for the weather, it's the microchip at work—translating binary instructions into seamless, human-friendly experiences.

Chapter 3

Inside the Microchip

Microchips—those tiny components quietly powering everything from smartphones and laptops to medical equipment and satellites—are modern marvels of engineering. At a glance, they may appear as nothing more than glossy, black rectangles soldered onto green circuit boards. But hidden beneath that unassuming exterior is a multilayered masterpiece of design, precision, and raw technological power.

The average person interacts with devices containing microchips hundreds of times per day, often without a second thought. We touch a phone screen, and it responds. We send a message, and it zips across the world in an instant. A car's engine adjusts its performance automatically, a smartwatch tracks heart rhythms, and a thermostat "learns" our preferences. In all these scenarios, the microchip is the silent force making it all possible.

To truly appreciate the power of a microchip, one must peer inside—far beyond the packaging, deep into the silicon where electrons race along hair-thin paths and make logic-based decisions in nanoseconds. This microscopic world is composed of meticulously arranged transistors, layered circuits, and interconnects so precise they challenge the limits of physics.

Unlike mechanical systems of the past, which relied on gears, levers, and rotary switches, microchips operate on a scale where components are measured in nanometers—a size comparison that makes even human hair seem gargantuan. Creating them requires environments free of dust and vibration, where the smallest impurity could ruin an entire batch of chips. Their manufacturing is among the most complex processes humans have ever developed, involving chemistry, physics, computer science, and artful engineering.

Yet despite their complexity, the design philosophy of microchips remains consistent: compact power, maximum efficiency, and unyielding reliability. The layers within a chip are not random or decorative—they're a carefully orchestrated structure, each one contributing to a specific function, whether it's storing information, executing instructions, or transmitting signals with precision timing.

Understanding what lies inside a microchip is like dissecting the brain of modern electronics. Each structural component tells a story of evolution—of how we went from bulky vacuum tubes to billions of microscopic transistors that turn on and off in billionths of a second. And as we explore this fascinating architecture, it becomes clear how foundational microchips are to everything around us—not just as hardware, but as the digital lifeblood of an increasingly intelligent world.

Structural Layers of a Microchip

At its core, a microchip is built in layers—delicate, microscopic strata that work in harmony to process, store, and relay digital information. These layers aren't stacked like a sandwich but rather intricately woven together using advanced fabrication techniques that have evolved over decades of innovation.

The foundation of nearly every microchip begins with a silicon wafer—a thin, circular slice of pure silicon, often measuring up to 300 millimeters in diameter. This base material is chosen for its excellent semiconductor properties, enabling it to control electrical conductivity with incredible precision. Silicon wafers are polished until mirror-smooth and serve as the canvas upon which countless tiny components are constructed.

Once the wafer is prepared, the deposition process begins. This involves adding various thin films of material—such as oxides, nitrides, and metals—each serving a unique function. For instance, silicon dioxide layers can act as insulators, while metal layers like copper and aluminum serve as conductors. These materials are either grown directly on the wafer or deposited using methods like chemical vapor deposition (CVD) or physical vapor deposition (PVD).

After deposition, engineers employ photolithography—a process that uses ultraviolet light and masks to etch intricate patterns onto the chip. This is how pathways and component outlines are drawn. A photoresist chemical is spread over the wafer, exposed to light through a mask, and then developed to reveal the underlying pattern. Areas unprotected by the photoresist are etched away with plasma or chemical solutions, forming the required shapes.

This is followed by ion implantation or doping, where specific elements like boron or phosphorus are embedded into the silicon to alter its electrical properties. These "doped" regions determine how transistors and other components behave, allowing engineers to create p-type or n-type semiconductors—crucial for building diodes and transistors.

After the structural base and electrical properties are defined, the chip moves into the metallization stage. This is where interconnects—the tiny highways that carry electrical signals—are added. These are made using ultra-fine metal lines and vias (vertical connections between layers) that form a multi-level network of conductive paths. In the most advanced chips, there can be more than 15 layers of these interconnects, each carefully aligned to ensure minimal resistance and maximum speed.

Between these layers, dielectric materials—essentially microscopic insulators—are inserted to prevent electrical interference and signal crosstalk. These materials also act as buffers, ensuring that electrical noise doesn't compromise the chip's operation. The arrangement of these materials must be so precise that any slight misalignment could cause cascading failures in logic processing or memory operations.

Each structural layer also contributes to the chip's ability to manage thermal performance. As components become denser, they generate more heat in smaller spaces. Special materials and architectural strategies are incorporated to disperse heat effectively, ensuring that the chip remains cool enough to function without degradation or failure.

By the time a chip is finished, it contains thousands of these meticulously crafted layers—some only a few atoms thick—working in perfect unison. It's an engineering achievement that requires atomic-level precision and collaboration between design teams, materials scientists, and manufacturing specialists. Every layer has a purpose. Every line is calculated. Every nanometer counts.

Transistor Technology: MOSFETs, FinFETs, and More

Transistors are the invisible workhorses inside every microchip. They don't move, buzz, or glow, but their actions are constant, swift, and precise. By flipping between on and off states, these minuscule devices perform the binary logic operations that drive computing, memory storage, and signal processing. In the early days of electronics, transistors were large enough to be seen and handled individually. Today, billions of them are crammed into a space smaller than a fingernail—each one engineered with such delicacy that they operate reliably despite being only a few nanometers in size.

At the heart of modern transistor technology lies the MOSFET, or Metal-Oxide-Semiconductor Field-Effect Transistor. It is the foundational building block of nearly every digital device in existence. A MOSFET works much like a switch—it can turn electrical current on or off based on the voltage applied to a gate terminal. Structurally, it consists of three terminals: the source, drain, and gate. When a voltage is applied to the gate, it creates an electric field that allows current to flow between the source and drain. This seemingly simple action—repeated billions of times per second—forms the basis for processing instructions and manipulating data in binary form.

What makes MOSFETs so powerful is their scalability and efficiency. They require very little power to operate and can be manufactured in extremely small sizes using photolithographic processes. As technology progressed, the size of these transistors has shrunk dramatically—moving from micrometers to nanometers. But this miniaturization brought its own challenges. As

MOSFETs became smaller, they started to suffer from leakage currents and short-channel effects, reducing their reliability and energy efficiency.

This is where FinFET technology emerged as a revolutionary solution. Short for Fin Field-Effect Transistor, the FinFET is a 3D transistor design introduced to overcome the limitations of traditional planar MOSFETs. Rather than lying flat on the silicon substrate, a FinFET's conducting channel stands upright, resembling a fin—hence the name. The gate wraps around the channel on three sides, offering better control over the flow of current and significantly reducing leakage.

FinFETs began to replace planar MOSFETs in mainstream semiconductor manufacturing around the 22-nanometer technology node. They offer improved performance at lower voltages, enabling faster switching speeds and more efficient power use—two critical requirements in today's battery-powered and high-performance devices. For instance, smartphones, which demand both powerful processing and long battery life, benefit immensely from FinFET integration.

In the relentless pursuit of even smaller and more efficient transistors, researchers and engineers have explored newer frontiers beyond FinFETs. One of the most promising innovations is Gate-All-Around FETs (GAAFETs). As the name suggests, this design allows the gate to surround the channel on all sides, providing unparalleled control over the transistor's behavior. GAAFETs are expected to be used in chips built on the 3-nan ometer node and beyond, pushing the limits of miniaturization and efficiency even further. This next-generation transistor is poised to revolutionize the semiconductor industry, enabling even more compact, energy-efficient, and powerful microchips for a variety of applications, from AI and quantum computing to next-gen mobile devices.

The transition to GAAFETs marks the next step in the evolution of transistors, and while this technology promises remarkable advancements, it also poses new challenges. For instance, the manufacturing of GAAFETs requires intricate precision and the development of advanced techniques in nanofabrication. Yet, as these hurdles are overcome, GAAFETs could pave the way for the next wave of innovation in the semiconductor industry.

Meanwhile, another area of intense focus is in the exploration of alternative materials for transistors, such as graphene and carbon nanotubes. These materials offer unique electrical properties that could, in theory, outperform silicon in terms of speed, conductivity, and power efficiency. While challenges still exist in integrating these materials into large-scale production, the potential for significant breakthroughs in transistor technology remains vast.

The continued evolution of transistor technologies like MOSFETs, FinFETs, and the emerging GAAFETs illustrates how semiconductor innovations will continue to meet the growing demands of faster, more efficient devices. With each breakthrough, the future of computing becomes more powerful, smaller, and energy-efficient, enabling innovations in fields like artificial intelligence, the Internet of Things (IoT), and beyond.

Interconnects, Memory Blocks, and Functional Units

Once the transistors are in place, another crucial aspect of a microchip's functionality is the interconnects—the wiring that forms the pathways for electrical signals to travel between transistors and other components. These interconnects create the intricate network that allows different parts of a microchip to communicate with each other and work together seamlessly to perform tasks. Without the interconnects, the billions of transistors on a chip would be isolated from one another, rendering the chip useless.

Interconnects are typically made of copper or aluminum, though copper is increasingly preferred due to its superior electrical conductivity. The interconnects are patterned onto the chip using a photolithographic process that creates thin, metallic layers connecting transistors, logic gates, and other components. These interconnects are often stacked in multiple layers, each layer consisting of a combination of metal lines and vias (vertical connections that link layers). As the chip size continues to shrink, managing the interconnects becomes more challenging, and special techniques such as low-k dielectric materials and through-silicon vias (TSVs) are employed to ensure signal integrity and minimize power loss due to resistance.

The process of connecting all these elements seamlessly is critical for microchips to operate at their full potential. Every nanometer of space must be precisely utilized, and ensuring that signals travel efficiently across the chip is essential for maintaining performance, especially as chips become more complex with increasing transistor density.

Next, we have the memory blocks, which serve as another key component of a microchip. Memory is what allows a chip to temporarily store data for quick access during operations. Modern microchips contain various types of memory blocks, each optimized for specific purposes. These can include volatile memory, such as DRAM (dynamic random-access memory), which is used to store data that can be quickly accessed and changed, and non-volatile memory, such as flash memory, which retains data even when power is removed.

A microchip's memory system is organized into hierarchies to balance speed and size. For instance, the most frequently accessed data is stored in cache memory, which is incredibly fast but relatively small in capacity. As the distance between the processor and the memory increases, the access speed generally decreases. This is why microchips are designed with multiple layers of memory, each progressively slower and larger in capacity. Cache memory is closest to the processor, followed by main memory (DRAM), and then secondary storage like hard drives or SSDs.

Alongside the memory blocks, a chip also contains functional units that are responsible for specific tasks such as arithmetic operations, logic processing, and data manipulation. These functional units include ALUs (Arithmetic Logic Units), which perform mathematical and logical operations, and FPUs (Floating Point Units), which are specialized for operations involving decimal numbers. The integration of these functional units allows a microchip to handle a wide variety of tasks simultaneously, performing complex computations, executing instructions, and facilitating communication between different components.

The interconnects, memory blocks, and functional units of a microchip work in concert, allowing the chip to carry out a wide range of tasks. When you use a smartphone, computer, or any other device that relies on microchips, you're benefiting from the incredible speed and efficiency of these systems. The faster the interconnects can move data between components, the quicker the memory can store and retrieve data, and the more capable the functional units are at executing instructions, the better the overall performance of the chip. In this way, every microchip is a masterpiece of engineering, with millions or billions of interconnected components working together to deliver performance.

Despite these advancements, the challenges of scaling microchips to smaller sizes continue to push the boundaries of what's possible. As we move towards more powerful and compact devices, engineers are exploring innovative materials and designs to ensure that future microchips continue to meet the ever-growing demands for speed, efficiency, and storage capacity.

Interconnects, Memory Blocks, and Functional Units

Inside a microchip, it's not just the transistors that do the work. The way these transistors are connected and the organization of different functional units determine how well a microchip performs its tasks. Interconnects, memory blocks, and various functional units work together to ensure that the chip operates smoothly, processes data effectively, and delivers performance on demand.

Interconnects are the pathways that link transistors together, enabling them to communicate with one another. These connections are made of tiny metal wires, often made from copper, which carry electrical signals across the chip. The efficiency of these interconnects is crucial—if the paths are too narrow or have poor conductivity, the signals can become delayed or corrupted, reducing the overall performance of the chip. As chips have become more advanced, the complexity of interconnects has increased exponentially. Advanced chips now feature multilayered interconnects that can pass signals through multiple levels of wiring, stacked in a vertical orientation, thus improving speed and density.

With this vast complexity, engineers face the challenge of ensuring that the interconnects don't interfere with each other or cause "crosstalk," where signals meant for one part of the chip leak into another. This is particularly important as chips become more densely packed with transistors and processing units. The challenge is exacerbated by the fact that electrical signals on these interconnects travel at a fraction of the speed of light, meaning that as the chips get faster, delays introduced by interconnects become a major bottleneck in performance.

Memory blocks inside a microchip are another essential element. Memory is where data is stored temporarily or permanently during processing. Microchips use different types of memory blocks, with each type designed for specific purposes. Some of the most common forms include volatile memory (which loses data when power is off) and non-volatile memory (which retains data without power). One of the most important types of memory in modern microchips is cache memory—a high-speed memory unit that stores frequently accessed data for quick retrieval, significantly improving overall processing speed.

Another crucial element is random-access memory (RAM), which allows the chip to access data in any order, making it an essential component for fast and responsive systems. RAM, however, is volatile, meaning that once the power is turned off, all data is lost. As such, non-volatile memories like flash memory are also critical for retaining data long-term, especially in devices like smartphones and computers, where data persistence is required.

Functional units within a microchip are specialized circuits designed to perform certain tasks. These units work by organizing and managing the flow of data across the chip, handling everything from arithmetic operations to input/output management. For example, an arithmetic logic unit (ALU) is a fundamental part of a processor's functional unit, capable of carrying out basic math operations like addition, subtraction, and multiplication. Similarly, a control unit (CU) directs the chip's operations, issuing instructions to other functional units and ensuring that all parts of the chip are synchronized and working together efficiently.

As chip designs evolve, engineers strive to balance complexity and performance. Functional units are becoming more specialized, allowing chips to carry out increasingly sophisticated tasks more efficiently. For example, graphics processing units (GPUs) are now integrated into many chips to accelerate visual computing tasks, while neural processing units (NPUs) are specialized for artificial intelligence (AI) workloads, processing vast amounts of data with incredible speed and low power consumption.

Moreover, high-bandwidth memory (HBM) is becoming an integral part of modern chips, especially in high-performance computing. HBM allows for rapid data transfer between memory and processing units, a necessity for tasks like video rendering, machine learning, and complex simulations.

The intricate relationship between interconnects, memory blocks, and functional units inside a microchip exemplifies the remarkable complexity of modern electronics.

As chips continue to shrink, each part must be meticulously designed and tested to ensure seamless communication and high performance.

Chapter 4

How Microchips Process Information

The process by which a microchip transforms raw data into meaningful output is both mesmerizing and invisible. Beneath the hard shell of every electronic device, a vibrant, silent dance of electrons unfolds—ordered, efficient, and lightning-fast. Microchips don't simply store or transmit data; they interpret it, manipulate it, calculate with it, and direct its flow, orchestrating complex operations within fractions of a second.

For most people, a smartphone opening a map application or a car's dashboard updating fuel efficiency numbers seems like magic. But deep within these experiences lies a tightly engineered structure of logic and synchronization that governs the movement of every bit and byte. Microchips function by implementing rules of logic derived from mathematics and physics, turning input into output through carefully designed circuits. Each flicker of electrical current follows a path that's been meticulously engineered to follow precise logical decisions—ones and zeros following invisible instructions.

Understanding how microchips process information requires a closer look at how digital systems operate in the first place. Unlike analog systems that vary continuously, digital systems operate in discrete steps, representing information in binary form. Every command, every keystroke, every video frame is translated into sequences of ones and zeros that are fed through microscopic networks of transistors. These transistors switch on and off, responding to signals and influencing the behavior of logic circuits that form the brain of the chip.

While the idea of processing information might seem abstract, it's grounded in physical structures built into the silicon of the chip. Gates, wires, transistors, memory units, and synchronization signals work in harmony to execute instructions from software. These instructions could be as simple as adding two numbers or as complex as rendering a 3D video scene. The speed at which this all happens is difficult to comprehend—billions of operations per second occur within a space smaller than a fingernail, without a single moving part.

Yet, raw speed alone is not what makes microchips powerful. It's their ability to coordinate, to follow step-by-step operations in a precisely timed sequence that allows complex tasks to be performed accurately. Microchips are not just about brute force computation; they're also about order, discipline, and structure. Timing, routing, and execution are just as important as computational power, and these are managed by deeply integrated mechanisms within the chip.

Consumers may never see the inner workings of a microchip, but they benefit from its performance in everyday life. Smooth video streaming, accurate GPS navigation, secure financial transactions, and even the functionality of life-saving medical devices all rely on microchips making rapid, reliable decisions. Each of these tasks stems from a carefully built architecture of logic and design—a microcosm of computation so compact and powerful that it's reshaping every corner of modern life.

With that foundation in mind, let's journey deeper into the core elements that make microchip processing possible.

Binary Logic and Digital Signals

In the world of microchips, everything begins with binary logic. This foundational principle allows complex systems to be built using only two states—on and off, or more technically, 1 and 0. These states form the building blocks of all digital information, from a simple character in a text message to the intricate visuals of a video game. What appears to the user as seamless digital interaction is, in fact, a symphony of binary operations happening at unimaginable speed.

Binary logic operates on the concept of voltage thresholds. When a transistor detects a voltage above a certain level, it interprets this as a binary "1"; when the voltage falls below that threshold, it reads a binary "0." This straightforward on/off mechanism enables precise and repeatable decision-making at the hardware level. It's elegant in its simplicity but astonishing in its power. A single binary digit, or bit, may seem insignificant, but in combination with billions of others, it forms the language through which microchips communicate and process the world around them.

What gives binary its strength is its compatibility with physical reality. It's easier and more reliable to distinguish between two states—high and low—than to maintain or interpret a continuous range of signals. This reliability makes binary ideal for electronic circuits, where interference, voltage drops, and noise can otherwise distort analog signals. With binary, as long as the signal crosses the threshold, the system will interpret it correctly—making it robust against many common forms of signal degradation.

Digital signals carry this binary information across the chip using electrical pulses. Each pulse represents a "1," while the absence of a pulse indicates a "0." These signals flow through copper or other conductive pathways, navigating a network of logic gates and throughout the journey to prevent corruption of data. Engineers go to great lengths to ensure that timing, resistance, and interference are carefully managed. A digital signal arriving a fraction too early or too late might lead to misinterpretation, causing errors in computation or system crashes. This is where timing precision becomes not just a preference, but a necessity—every nanosecond counts.

In more complex chips, these binary signals are managed using a variety of techniques to ensure that they remain synchronized and don't interfere with each other. Signal routing is optimized for efficiency and reliability, using multiple layers of interconnects that crisscross like miniature highways inside the chip. These electrical signals travel at near the speed of light, but they must be coordinated precisely to align with the chip's logic structure. Imagine a symphony orchestra where every musician must play their note at the exact right moment. The conductor, in this case, is the chip's internal clock and control units.

Another powerful feature of digital logic is its ability to scale. A single logic operation may not do much, but by combining millions or billions of them, microchips can execute extraordinarily complex instructions. This modularity allows for the creation of programmable processors, where software can dictate the behavior of the chip, instructing it to perform tasks ranging from image processing to artificial intelligence. And at the core of it all remains the same simple binary foundation—high or low, 1 or 0.

This efficient and fault-tolerant method of representing and transferring information is the backbone of all modern computing. Whether it's a calculator or a self-driving car, the principles of binary logic and digital signals enable machines to make decisions, solve problems, and communicate with other systems. And because these foundations are rooted in physical hardware, they provide a reliable and fast platform upon which more advanced systems are built.

Understanding this binary world is essential for appreciating just how far technology has come. From the earliest vacuum tube computers to today's highly integrated microprocessors, the power of the binary system has remained constant. What has changed is the scale, the speed, and the sophistication with which these binary decisions are made. In the next section, we explore how logic gates—simple digital switches—combine to form circuits that perform the computations at the heart of every digital device.

Logic Gates and Circuits Performing Computations

Logic gates are the microscopic decision-makers within every microchip. They are built from transistors and are responsible for implementing the basic operations of binary logic: AND, OR, NOT, XOR, NAND, and NOR. Each gate receives one or more binary inputs and produces a binary output according to a logical rule. For instance, an AND gate outputs a "1" only if all its inputs are "1," while a NOT gate simply inverts the input, turning a "1" into a "0" and vice versa.

Although each individual gate performs a very basic function, when combined, these gates create circuits that can execute incredibly complex operations. These include arithmetic calculations, memory management, decision-making, and data comparison—essentially all the activities that define computation.

One of the most familiar applications of logic gates is in arithmetic circuits. These circuits are designed to carry out addition, subtraction, multiplication, and division using binary numbers. For example, a half-adder is a simple circuit made from an XOR gate and an AND gate, capable of adding two single-bit binary numbers and generating a sum and a carry bit. Expand that design to include more gates, and you create a full adder, which can handle multiple-bit addition—a building block of any digital calculator or processor.

Multiplexers, demultiplexers, encoders, and decoders are other essential circuits constructed from logic gates. A multiplexer selects one of several input signals and forwards it to a single output line, acting as a sort of digital switchboard. Meanwhile, decoders do the reverse—converting coded binary input into a series of outputs. These components play a pivotal role in directing the flow of information through a chip, ensuring that the right operations happen at the right time and place.

Beyond arithmetic and routing, logic circuits also form the basis of memory and storage elements. Flip-flops, which are bistable circuits built from gates, serve as one-bit memory cells. They can store a value indefinitely, until changed by an input signal. Arrays of flip-flops and related structures are used to build the registers and memory cells that hold data temporarily while the processor works on it.

Logic circuits are also responsible for comparisons and conditionals—deciding whether one value is greater than another or if two values are equal. These functions are essential for software control flow, such as deciding whether a loop should continue or which instruction to execute next. In a sense, logic gates are the neurons of a computer—simple on their own, but capable of astonishing feats when interconnected.

As chip designs have become more sophisticated, engineers have developed entire logic blocks that perform standard functions. These reusable blocks, sometimes called IP cores, allow designers to assemble complex chips more quickly and reliably. They include pre-built logic for handling video, audio, networking, and encryption—all made possible through combinations of simple logic gates.

At the heart of all these operations is the coordination between logic gates to follow precise instructions, issued by the software and interpreted by the chip's control unit. These gates fire in sequences dictated by both the clock and the control signals, creating a dynamic and flexible processing environment. And though the gates are invisible to the human eye, their effects are all around us—in every search query, every automated process, every digital transaction.

Next, we'll explore how the microchip's core components—the arithmetic logic unit and the control unit—collaborate to carry out these binary-based operations with incredible speed and accuracy.

throughout the journey to prevent corruption of data. Engineers go to great lengths to ensure that timing, resistance, and interference are carefully managed. A digital signal arriving a fraction too early or too late might lead to misinterpretation, causing errors in computation or system crashes. This is where timing precision becomes not just a preference, but a necessity—every nanosecond counts.

In more complex chips, these binary signals are managed using a variety of techniques to ensure that they remain synchronized and don't interfere with each other. Signal routing is optimized for efficiency and reliability, using multiple layers of interconnects that crisscross like miniature highways inside the chip. These electrical signals travel at near the speed of light, but they must be coordinated precisely to align with the chip's logic structure. Imagine a symphony orchestra where every musician must play their note at the exact right moment. The conductor, in this case, is the chip's internal clock and control units.

Another powerful feature of digital logic is its ability to scale. A single logic operation may not do much, but by combining millions or billions of them, microchips can execute extraordinarily complex instructions. This modularity allows for the creation of programmable processors, where software can dictate the behavior of the chip, instructing it to perform tasks ranging from image processing to artificial intelligence. And at the core of it all remains the same simple binary foundation—high or low, 1 or 0.

This efficient and fault-tolerant method of representing and transferring information is the backbone of all modern computing. Whether it's a calculator or a self-driving car, the principles of binary logic and digital signals enable machines to make decisions, solve problems, and communicate with other systems. And because these foundations are rooted in physical hardware, they provide a reliable and fast platform upon which more advanced systems are built.

Understanding this binary world is essential for appreciating just how far technology has come. From the earliest vacuum tube computers to today's highly integrated microprocessors, the power of the binary system has remained constant. What has changed is the scale, the speed, and the sophistication with which these binary decisions are made. In the next section, we explore how logic gates—simple digital switches—combine to form circuits that perform the computations at the heart of every digital device.

Logic Gates and Circuits Performing Computations

Logic gates are the microscopic decision-makers within every microchip. They are built from transistors and are responsible for implementing the basic operations of binary logic: AND, OR, NOT, XOR, NAND, and NOR. Each gate receives one or more binary inputs and produces a binary output according to a logical rule. For instance, an AND gate outputs a "1" only if all its inputs are "1," while a NOT gate simply inverts the input, turning a "1" into a "0" and vice versa.

Although each individual gate performs a very basic function, when combined, these gates create circuits that can execute incredibly complex operations. These include arithmetic calculations, memory management, decision-making, and data comparison—essentially all the activities that define computation.

One of the most familiar applications of logic gates is in arithmetic circuits. These circuits are designed to carry out addition, subtraction, multiplication, and division using binary numbers. For example, a half-adder is a simple circuit made from an XOR gate and an AND gate, capable of adding two single-bit binary numbers and generating a sum and a carry bit. Expand that design to include more gates, and you create a full adder, which can handle multiple-bit addition—a building block of any digital calculator or processor.

Multiplexers, demultiplexers, encoders, and decoders are other essential circuits constructed from logic gates. A multiplexer selects one of several input signals and forwards it to a single output line, acting as a sort of digital switchboard. Meanwhile, decoders do the reverse—converting coded binary input into a series of outputs. These components play a pivotal role in directing the flow of information through a chip, ensuring that the right operations happen at the right time and place.

Beyond arithmetic and routing, logic circuits also form the basis of memory and storage elements. Flip-flops, which are bistable circuits built from gates, serve as one-bit memory cells. They can store a value indefinitely, until changed by an input signal. Arrays of flip-flops and related structures are used to build the registers and memory cells that hold data temporarily while the processor works on it.

Logic circuits are also responsible for comparisons and conditionals—deciding whether one value is greater than another or if two values are equal. These functions are essential for software control flow, such as deciding whether a loop should continue or which instruction to execute next. In a sense, logic gates are the neurons of a computer—simple on their own, but capable of astonishing feats when interconnected.

As chip designs have become more sophisticated, engineers have developed entire logic blocks that perform standard functions. These reusable blocks, sometimes called IP cores, allow designers to assemble complex chips more quickly and reliably. They include pre-built logic for handling video, audio, networking, and encryption—all made possible through combinations of simple logic gates.

At the heart of all these operations is the coordination between logic gates to follow precise instructions, issued by the software and interpreted by the chip's control unit. These gates fire in sequences dictated by both the clock and the control signals, creating a dynamic and flexible processing environment. And though the gates are invisible to the human eye, their effects are all around us—in every search query, every automated process, every digital transaction.

Next, we'll explore how the microchip's core components—the arithmetic logic unit and the control unit—collaborate to carry out these binary-based operations with incredible speed and accuracy.

The Role of the Arithmetic Logic Unit and Control Unit

Inside every microchip, two critical components work in tandem to turn binary instructions into purposeful action: the Arithmetic Logic Unit (ALU) and the Control Unit (CU). These units form the bedrock of a processor's decision-making and computing capabilities.

The ALU is the engine of computation. It's responsible for carrying out basic arithmetic operations—such as addition, subtraction, multiplication, and division—as well as logical operations like AND, OR, NOT, and XOR. When a device adds numbers in a spreadsheet, compares two values in a game, or evaluates conditional logic in an app, it's the ALU doing the heavy lifting. It handles all of this with binary precision, using logic gates built from transistors to manipulate bits.

Yet, the ALU doesn't act independently. It relies on the Control Unit to tell it what to do and when. The Control Unit is like the conductor of an orchestra, ensuring every part of the microchip works in sync. It decodes the instructions fetched from memory, interprets what action should be taken, and sends out control signals that activate the appropriate components—including the ALU.

Together, these two units create the harmony that powers all digital devices. The ALU handles the core computations, while the Control Unit orchestrates the overall flow—fetching instructions, interpreting them, and managing the execution sequence. Without them, software would remain nothing more than static code, incapable of influencing the world around it.

Clock Cycles and Synchronization

All the precise operations within a microchip—from basic math to complex program logic—depend on a steady rhythm, maintained by the clock cycle. This internal clock acts as the heartbeat of the processor, ticking at billions of cycles per second and ensuring that all parts of the chip remain perfectly in sync.

Each clock cycle is a pulse—a transition in voltage that tells the microchip it's time to perform the next small task. Think of it as a stopwatch that triggers every action inside the chip, from fetching an instruction to writing a result to memory. The faster the clock ticks, the more operations the chip can complete in a given time. A 2 GHz processor, for instance, executes two billion such pulses every second.

But speed isn't everything. Synchronization is just as important. The clock ensures that all parts of the chip—ALU, memory, registers, buses—coordinate their actions precisely. This coordination prevents errors like data being written too early or calculations being performed before the required values are available.

In more advanced chips, features like pipelining and parallelism allow multiple instructions to be processed simultaneously. This makes synchronization even more vital. Each pipeline stage relies on accurate timing to avoid overlaps, stalls, or corruption of data. The clock signal, synchronized across the entire chip, is what makes this possible.

Without the clock cycle, the microchip would be a chaotic collection of parts. With it, every component falls into rhythm, executing billions of tiny steps that culminate in the seamless digital experiences we depend on daily.

Data Paths, Bus Systems, and Execution Flow

If the ALU and Control Unit are the brain and logic of the chip, then the data paths and bus systems are its circulatory system—moving information from one part of the processor to another with speed and precision.

A data path is the route that data follows as it moves through the microchip. It consists of several key elements: registers that temporarily store data, multiplexers that direct traffic, buses that serve as data highways, and logic units that transform the data as needed. This path is carefully constructed to allow quick and efficient access to operands, as well as fast delivery of results.

The bus system is a shared set of connections that allows different components of the chip to communicate. There are typically three main types of buses:

Data Bus: Transfers actual binary data between the CPU, memory, and other peripherals.

Address Bus: Carries memory addresses that tell the system where data should be read from or written to.

Control Bus: Sends control signals that manage operations like reading, writing, and signaling when tasks are complete.

All these buses work in unison under the direction of the Control Unit. When an instruction is ready to execute, the CU sends signals through the control bus, telling the ALU what kind of operation to perform and directing data along the proper paths. The address bus identifies where the required data lives in memory, while the data bus carries it to the ALU for processing. Once complete, the result travels back along the data path to its destination.

The execution flow—the step-by-step process of instruction handling—is built on top of these systems. It typically follows a cycle: fetch the instruction from memory, decode it to determine the task, execute the operation using the ALU, and then store the result. This cycle happens billions of times per second, with data whizzing through the chip's highways in perfect coordination.

Thanks to this intricate web of paths, buses, and control signals, the chip can translate software commands into real-world outcomes—calculations, animations, user interactions, and everything in between.

Chapter 5

How Microchips Are Made

The magic behind every microchip starts long before it's ever placed into a smartphone, a car, or any of the other devices we use daily. The creation of these tiny, complex pieces of technology is a feat of engineering, chemistry, and physics that takes place in state-of-the-art facilities, where every step is meticulously designed to achieve the precision required for a functional microchip. At the heart of this process is the transformation of raw materials into intricate structures that can perform billions of operations per second, making our modern digital world possible.

The journey from concept to chip involves many steps, each of which requires extreme attention to detail and careful planning. It begins with the selection of the right materials, then moves to the actual fabrication of the chip through highly specialized processes that are guided by the principles of physics and chemistry. Every microchip is crafted in a controlled environment to ensure the highest level of precision, where even the smallest error can render an entire batch useless. To the untrained eye, it might seem like a simple product, but it's the result of years of research, precision engineering, and advanced manufacturing techniques.

Understanding the full scope of how microchips are made requires a closer look at the materials, steps, and technologies that go into their production. From selecting the right semiconductor materials to the nanometer precision of cleanroom environments, each step is a critical part of creating these essential components. In this chapter, we explore how a raw piece of silicon becomes the powerful microchip that runs your devices, and how manufacturers deal with the challenges of producing them at scale.

Semiconductor Materials and Properties

The heart of any microchip lies in its core material: **semiconductors**. These materials possess unique properties that allow them to control the flow of electricity—an essential function in modern electronics. A semiconductor's ability to act as both a conductor and an insulator makes it perfect for controlling electrical current, which is fundamental for microchips to perform complex calculations and data processing.

The most common semiconductor material used in microchip manufacturing is **silicon**, a naturally abundant element that's easy to refine and has ideal electrical properties for most applications. Silicon is neither a perfect conductor nor a perfect insulator, but it can be precisely controlled to how microchips are made, aligned with your preferences.

Chip Packaging and Testing

After the microchip has been fabricated and the individual circuits have been created through processes like photolithography, doping, etching, and layering, the next major stage is chip packaging. This step is crucial as it determines how the chip will interact with other components in the device. Without packaging, the fragile circuits of the microchip would be exposed to damage and could not be properly integrated into a device.

Chip packaging involves enclosing the microchip in a protective case, which also serves to facilitate its connection to other electronic components. The chip is first attached to a substrate, a material that provides physical support and acts as an interface between the microchip and the external world. The chip is then connected to the substrate through fine wires that bridge the gap between the chip's pins and the substrate's leads.

Once the connections are made, the chip is encased in a plastic or ceramic package that helps protect it from physical and environmental damage. This package often includes features like heat sinks, which help to dissipate the heat generated by the microchip during operation, as well as electrical contacts for connecting the chip to other components in the device, such as memory or power systems.

Testing is an integral part of this process. After packaging, the chip undergoes functional testing to ensure that it operates as expected. This testing includes checking the chip's ability to process data, handle power, and connect with other components. Chips that fail to meet these rigorous standards are discarded, which is a critical part of maintaining quality control in the manufacturing process.

Once a chip has passed all tests, it is ready to be distributed for use in consumer electronics, automotive systems, or industrial applications. However, even after it has passed testing, manufacturers must continually monitor the performance of the chips in real-world applications to identify any potential issues or defects that may not have been caught during the initial tests. This ongoing monitoring helps improve future production processes and ensure the continued reliability of microchips.

Yield, Defects, and Mass Production Strategies

The process of making microchips is highly sophisticated, and with such complexity comes the inevitable challenge of ensuring that every chip produced meets the required standards. As chips are so intricate, the production process is inherently prone to defects. These defects can occur at any point in the fabrication process and can arise from even the smallest variations in materials, equipment, or environmental conditions. Therefore, yield—the percentage of functional chips produced compared to the total number of chips fabricated—is a critical metric in semiconductor manufacturing.

Microchip manufacturers invest heavily in technology and systems that allow them to detect and mitigate defects. During the fabrication process, chips are constantly inspected for defects such as patterning errors, contamination, and misalignments that can cause failure. Even the tiniest flaw can make a chip unusable, so ensuring high yield is a major priority. In many cases, defects are corrected by carefully adjusting the fabrication parameters or implementing more precise equipment. However, despite all efforts, some defects are inevitable due to the scale and complexity of the process.

In response to the challenge of defects, manufacturers implement mass production strategies aimed at maximizing efficiency and minimizing the impact of defects. One of the most common strategies is the use of multi-layered chips. By building multiple layers of circuits on a single silicon wafer, manufacturers increase the chances of producing multiple good chips, even if some of the layers are defective. Another strategy is the use of wafer binning, where the wafers are sorted by quality, and chips that meet specific criteria are set aside for high-end applications, while lower-quality chips are used for less demanding applications.

The challenge of maintaining high yields is compounded by the continuous demand for smaller, faster, and more energy-efficient chips. As the industry continues to push the boundaries of microchip technology, manufacturers must constantly refine their processes to ensure that they can produce chips that meet the ever-growing demands of the digital world.

Despite the challenges, the mass production of microchips is a critical part of the global technology ecosystem. Every year, billions of chips are produced, powering everything from smartphones and computers to home appliances and automobiles. The ability to produce these chips at scale, while maintaining a high level of quality, is a testament to the incredible advances in semiconductor manufacturing technologies.

Chapter 6

Types of Microchips and Their Roles

The digital landscape is powered by a variety of microchips, each designed with a specific role in mind. These chips are the invisible workhorses behind nearly every modern electronic device, from mobile phones and laptops to industrial robots and satellites. They don't just enable functionality—they define it. Without the right chip architecture, even the most powerful software would have no foundation to run on. Understanding the different types of microchips and their unique functions opens a window into how devices operate, how tasks are optimized, and how innovation continues to reshape the digital world.

Every device, from a smartwatch to a supercomputer, contains one or more types of microchips working in tandem. Some chips focus on computation, others on data storage, and still others on managing specialized tasks like image rendering or communication with sensors. The diversity of these chips reflects the complexity of modern technology. As systems evolve, microchips are increasingly designed to work together in highly integrated environments, optimizing both performance and energy efficiency. The following sections explore the most essential categories of microchips and the roles they play in today's technological ecosystem.

Central Processing Units (CPUs)

The central processing unit, commonly referred to as the CPU, is often likened to the brain of any computing device. It's responsible for executing instructions, performing calculations, and managing tasks that drive the entire system. From opening a file to running complex algorithms, the CPU orchestrates these actions through a blend of speed, architecture, and precision.

At its core, the CPU is built around a few key components: the arithmetic logic unit (ALU) for performing mathematical and logical operations, the control unit (CU) that interprets instructions and directs other components, and registers for temporary data storage. These elements work in concert, synchronized by clock signals, to ensure the system operates efficiently and accurately.

CPUs are built to be general-purpose and flexible, capable of handling a wide variety of tasks. This versatility is why they're found in nearly every kind of device. In personal computers and servers, CPUs are the primary engines behind everything from browsing the web to rendering spreadsheets and running software applications.

Modern CPUs are multi-core, meaning they contain multiple processing units within a single chip. This allows for parallel processing, where tasks are split across cores for faster execution. Clock speed, measured in gigahertz (GHz), indicates how many cycles a CPU can perform per second, but overall performance depends on many other factors, including cache size, instruction set efficiency, and thermal management.

The importance of CPUs cannot be overstated. Whether embedded in consumer electronics, powering enterprise-grade servers, or managing industrial automation, the CPU remains central to digital computing. Its design continues to evolve, with newer architectures incorporating artificial intelligence capabilities, advanced power efficiency, and integration with other specialized chips for more balanced performance.

Graphics Processing Units (GPUs)

Graphics processing units, or GPUs, have transformed from their origins as video rendering engines into computational powerhouses used in a wide range of applications. Initially developed to accelerate image and video processing, GPUs are now essential in fields such as artificial intelligence, machine learning, scientific simulations, and even cryptocurrency mining.

What makes GPUs unique is their architecture. Unlike CPUs, which have a few powerful cores optimized for sequential processing, GPUs consist of hundreds or even thousands of smaller cores designed for parallel processing. This allows them to execute thousands of operations simultaneously, making them ideal for tasks that require processing large blocks of data at once—like rendering images or running neural networks.

In gaming, GPUs enable lifelike graphics by handling real-time rendering, shading, and texture mapping. In professional settings, such as animation studios or CAD systems, high-performance GPUs accelerate workloads that would be too slow for CPUs alone. In scientific computing, GPUs assist in processing vast datasets for simulations, such as climate modeling or molecular research.

The rise of AI and machine learning has given GPUs a renewed spotlight. Their ability to train deep learning models at high speed makes them indispensable in data centers and research labs. Many frameworks, such as TensorFlow and PyTorch, are optimized for GPU acceleration to achieve faster results.

GPUs now often exist as dedicated cards (discrete GPUs) or integrated within the same chip as the CPU (integrated GPUs). Discrete GPUs offer more power and are typically used in high-end systems, while integrated ones provide cost and power efficiency for everyday computing needs.

As tasks become more data-intensive and visually complex, the GPU's role in modern computing continues to expand. It's not just about graphics anymore—it's about high-performance computation in an increasingly visual and intelligent digital world.

Memory Chips: DRAM, SRAM, ROM, and Flash

Memory chips serve as the short-term and long-term storage hubs within any electronic device. While the CPU and GPU perform computations, memory chips hold the data and instructions these processors need to operate efficiently. Several types of memory exist, each tailored to a specific need, and understanding their differences is essential for appreciating how digital systems function.

Dynamic RAM (DRAM) is the most common type of system memory in computers. It stores data in capacitors that must be refreshed thousands of times per second to retain information. DRAM is valued for its high density and relatively low cost, making it ideal for providing the main memory in desktops, laptops, and servers.

Static RAM (SRAM), on the other hand, is faster and more reliable because it doesn't require constant refreshing. Instead of using capacitors, it uses flip-flops to store data, which makes it more power-hungry and expensive. SRAM is typically used in cache memory, where speed is paramount.

Read-Only Memory (ROM) holds data that doesn't change, such as firmware—the low-level software that initializes hardware during boot-up. Unlike RAM, ROM retains its content even when power is removed. Manufacturers program ROM during production, and it's essential for foundational operations in embedded systems and computing devices.

Flash memory bridges the gap between volatile RAM and permanent storage. It's a type of EEPROM (Electrically Erasable Programmable Read-Only Memory) that allows data to be written and erased in blocks. Flash is used in USB drives, SSDs (Solid State Drives), smartphones, and memory cards. Its non-volatile nature means it retains data without power, and it's fast enough to support real-time access in many applications.

Each of these memory types plays a vital role in system performance. DRAM handles fast-access tasks, SRAM supports ultra-fast temporary storage, ROM secures essential boot data, and flash provides durable, high-capacity storage for everyday use. Together, they form a dynamic network of memory systems that keep devices responsive, efficient, and reliable.

Microcontrollers and Embedded Systems

Microcontrollers are compact computing systems designed to manage specific tasks within embedded systems. Unlike general-purpose CPUs, microcontrollers come integrated with memory, input/output peripherals, and often even timers or communication modules—all on a single chip. They're the silent controllers behind everything from microwave ovens to automobile engine systems.

An embedded system refers to any device that uses a microcontroller to perform dedicated functions within a larger system. These systems are purpose-built, meaning they're designed to do a specific job—such as monitoring temperature, controlling motors, or processing sensor inputs—rather than running a wide range of applications like a smartphone or laptop.

Microcontrollers are valued for their low power consumption, reliability, and cost efficiency. They can operate for years on small batteries and are built to endure demanding environments. In industrial automation, for example, microcontrollers oversee machinery operations, monitor safety systems, and relay sensor data to control units.

One of the most recognizable features of microcontrollers is their use in the Internet of Things (IoT). Devices such as smart thermostats, fitness trackers, and security systems rely on microcontrollers to process data locally and communicate with cloud platforms. Their ability to deliver localized intelligence with minimal energy requirements makes them ideal for IoT applications.

While they may not match the speed or flexibility of larger processors, microcontrollers are optimized for real-time control and reliability. They run firmware—streamlined code designed to execute quickly and without fail. This specialization allows embedded systems to function with remarkable consistency, even in critical roles like medical devices, automotive safety systems, or industrial controls.

The combination of integration, simplicity, and endurance makes microcontrollers a cornerstone of modern electronics. They empower devices to be smart, autonomous, and connected in ways that continue to reshape everyday life.

ASICs, FPGAs, and SoCs

The semiconductor world is not limited to general-purpose chips. For specialized needs, designers turn to custom and semi-custom solutions such as ASICs, FPGAs, and SoCs. These chips are tailored to specific applications and offer distinct advantages in speed, efficiency, and versatility.

Application-Specific Integrated Circuits (ASICs) are chips designed to perform a particular function or set of functions with maximum efficiency. They are highly optimized, which means they can outperform general-purpose processors in speed and power consumption. ASICs are widely used in consumer electronics, telecommunications, and even cryptocurrency mining, where performance and efficiency are critical. However, they are expensive and time-consuming to design, making them suitable only for high-volume production.

Field-Programmable Gate Arrays (FPGAs) offer a flexible alternative. Unlike ASICs, FPGAs can be reprogrammed after manufacturing, allowing developers to customize their functionality based on application needs. They are ideal for prototyping, custom hardware implementations, and industries that require rapid iteration or hardware adaptability. FPGAs are commonly used in aerospace, defense, and medical applications where conditions and requirements may change over time.

System-on-Chip (SoC) represents the pinnacle of integration. An SoC includes a CPU, GPU, memory, communication interfaces, and other peripherals—all on a single silicon chip. This design allows for compact, energy-efficient systems that still deliver high performance. SoCs are the foundation of smartphones, tablets, and many embedded devices. Their all-in-one nature simplifies design, reduces costs, and improves efficiency.

While each of these chip types serves a different purpose, they all contribute to expanding the capabilities of digital systems. ASICs maximize performance for specific tasks, FPGAs deliver reconfigurable logic for dynamic applications, and SoCs consolidate complex systems into compact, efficient packages. These innovations enable modern technology to become more powerful, adaptable, and accessible than ever before.

Chapter 7

Microchips in Everyday Life

Microchips have become the silent orchestrators of modern life, woven into the fabric of our daily routines. Their presence is nearly invisible, yet their impact is profound—transforming how we communicate, travel, work, heal, and even secure our identities. Far from being confined to computers or specialized machinery, microchips have expanded their reach to nearly every object that plugs in, powers up, or connects online.

Whether tucked inside a smartwatch monitoring heartbeats or buried deep within an automated assembly line, microchips deliver speed, intelligence, and control. Their ability to process, store, and communicate data has allowed everyday tools to evolve into smart, responsive companions. The following sections reveal how microchips are reshaping the way we live, one device at a time.

Consumer Electronics: Smartphones, Tablets, and Wearables

Nowhere is the presence of microchips more tangible than in the devices we carry and wear each day. Smartphones, tablets, and wearables are microchip-driven marvels, designed to pack immense computing power into compact, portable frames.

Inside a typical smartphone lies a system-on-chip (SoC) that combines a CPU, GPU, memory controller, modem, and more. This integration allows smartphones to perform tasks that once required a full desktop computer—capturing high-resolution video, editing documents, navigating via GPS, and managing communication across multiple networks.

Tablets follow a similar blueprint, often using enhanced SoCs to support larger displays and extended functionality like digital drawing, multitasking, or media streaming. These devices rely on efficient microchip design to balance power and battery life without compromising performance.

Wearables such as smartwatches and fitness trackers use microcontrollers and low-power SoCs to monitor biometrics, track activity, and connect wirelessly to other devices. These microchips process sensor data in real time, enabling features like heart rate monitoring, sleep tracking, and step counting. The compact form factor demands extreme power efficiency and thermal management, challenges that chipmakers continue to address with innovation.

As consumer expectations grow, so does the sophistication of microchips. Advanced signal processing, AI capabilities, and enhanced wireless communication modules are becoming standard. These enhancements are pushing the boundaries of what mobile and wearable devices can accomplish, ensuring they remain essential companions in our increasingly connected lives.

Automotive Applications and Smart Vehicles

Microchips are redefining the concept of the automobile. Cars today are no longer just mechanical machines—they are intelligent systems on wheels, powered by hundreds of specialized chips that manage safety, navigation, performance, and entertainment.

Electronic Control Units (ECUs) are at the heart of automotive intelligence. These embedded microcontrollers monitor and control everything from engine timing and fuel injection to transmission and braking systems. By analyzing real-time sensor input, ECUs adjust vehicle behavior to optimize performance, fuel efficiency, and emissions control.

Modern vehicles are equipped with Advanced Driver-Assistance Systems (ADAS), which use microchips to interpret data from radar, cameras, ultrasonic sensors, and LiDAR systems. These chips enable features such as lane-keeping assistance, adaptive cruise control, and emergency braking—all of which enhance driver safety and pave the way for autonomous vehicles.

In electric vehicles (EVs), microchips oversee battery management systems, inverter control, and power distribution. They play a vital role in regulating energy flow and ensuring thermal balance. As EV adoption rises, the demand for highly efficient and durable chips grows in tandem.

Infotainment systems, GPS navigation, voice recognition, and wireless connectivity are also powered by microchips. These systems offer drivers and passengers seamless access to real-time traffic, streaming content, and smartphone integration—all managed through robust SoCs and dedicated processors.

The evolution toward smart vehicles and connected cars is driven by the need for real-time data processing, secure communication, and software upgradability—all areas where microchips are critical. As autonomous driving becomes more viable, the automotive industry's reliance on high-performance chips will only deepen.

Industrial Control Systems and Robotics

Behind every automated factory and smart production line lies a dense network of microchips coordinating the dance of machines. In industrial settings, microchips manage process control, data acquisition, and robotic movement—ensuring precision, safety, and efficiency at scale.

Programmable Logic Controllers (PLCs), built on robust microcontrollers or embedded processors, control machinery and production lines. These chips handle input from sensors, execute real-time logic, and issue commands to actuators, motors, and valves. Their rugged design allows them to withstand harsh environments and continuous operation.

Industrial robots are powered by a complex system of microchips managing motor control, spatial awareness, and object recognition. Microchips interpret feedback from position sensors and cameras to guide robotic arms with millimeter accuracy. In fields like automotive manufacturing, electronics assembly, and pharmaceuticals, robots driven by intelligent chips perform tasks faster and more consistently than human workers.

Data acquisition and monitoring systems use analog-to-digital converters and embedded processors to collect and process information from temperature sensors, pressure gauges, and flow meters. These microchips enable predictive maintenance, quality control, and energy management by turning raw data into actionable insights.

With the rise of Industry 4.0, microchips are also key to enabling machine-to-machine communication, remote diagnostics, and cloud integration. They allow factories to become adaptive, self-regulating environments capable of responding to changes in supply and demand in real time.

Medical Technology and Healthcare Devices

Microchips have revolutionized healthcare by powering devices that diagnose, monitor, and treat patients with unprecedented accuracy and efficiency. Whether embedded in wearable monitors or implanted within the human body, these chips bring intelligence and connectivity to the frontlines of medicine.

Diagnostic tools like portable ultrasound machines, MRI scanners, and glucose monitors rely on microchips for image processing, data interpretation, and wireless data sharing. These devices reduce the need for hospital visits and enable faster, more informed decisions by healthcare providers.

Implantable devices such as pacemakers and insulin pumps use microcontrollers to deliver precise therapy based on real-time physiological input. These chips are engineered for long-term reliability and biocompatibility, often operating for years without replacement.

Telemedicine tools—from remote monitoring kits to smart pill dispensers—use microchips to gather patient data and transmit it securely to healthcare professionals. They allow for continuous care beyond the clinic, improving outcomes for patients with chronic conditions or limited mobility.

In surgical environments, robotic-assisted systems guided by microchips enhance precision, reduce invasiveness, and shorten recovery times. These systems rely on real-time control loops, advanced imaging processors, and tactile feedback mechanisms to support surgeons during complex procedures.

Microchips also play a vital role in healthcare data systems, securing patient records, supporting diagnostics via AI algorithms, and facilitating digital workflows in hospitals. As personalized medicine advances, microchips will increasingly drive systems that tailor treatment to each individual's genetic and physiological profile.

Financial Systems and Identification Tools

Microchips are at the core of secure financial transactions and identity verification systems, enabling trust in an increasingly digital economy. From the chip embedded in your credit card to biometric ID scanners at airports, these technologies depend on reliable, tamper-proof microchips.

Smart cards, used in banking and access control, contain embedded chips that securely store data and perform cryptographic operations. These chips use secure elements and encryption algorithms to prevent fraud, counterfeit, or unauthorized access. Unlike magnetic stripes, smart card chips offer enhanced security by generating dynamic data for each transaction.

Point-of-sale terminals and ATMs are equipped with microchips to process payment authorizations and manage communication with banking networks. These processors verify user identity, execute encryption protocols, and store temporary transaction data—all in real time.

Biometric systems for facial recognition, fingerprint scanning, and iris recognition rely on microchips to process and match biometric data quickly and accurately. These chips support both local processing and secure transmission of biometric profiles to cloud databases.

In digital identity systems, microchips store personal information on e-passports, national ID cards, and driver's licenses. These chips not only hold data but also run secure applications that authenticate identity across borders and institutions.

The financial sector's shift toward contactless payments, digital wallets, and blockchain-based transactions continues to drive demand for microchips that deliver secure, fast, and scalable processing. As fraud techniques evolve, chip technology remains the first line of defense.

Internet of Things (IoT) Integration

Microchips are the heartbeat of the Internet of Things (IoT)—a vast and growing network of connected devices that communicate, automate, and learn. From smart homes to smart cities, the IoT ecosystem depends on microchips that enable sensing, processing, and wireless communication.

IoT devices embed microcontrollers and communication chips (Wi-Fi, Bluetooth, Zigbee, LoRa, or 5G) to collect environmental data, execute local decisions, and transmit information to cloud services. These chips are optimized for low power consumption, compact size, and real-time responsiveness.

Smart home appliances, such as thermostats, lights, security systems, and voice assistants, use microchips to adapt behavior based on user preferences, routines, and environmental cues. Chips enable these devices to communicate with each other and with smartphones, creating personalized, automated living spaces.

In smart agriculture, microchips monitor soil moisture, temperature, and nutrient levels, optimizing irrigation and fertilization through real-time analysis. In smart cities, embedded chips manage street lighting, traffic control, and waste collection to improve efficiency and reduce environmental impact.

Industrial IoT (IIoT) applications use chips for asset tracking, remote machine diagnostics, and supply chain visibility. These devices generate actionable insights, reduce downtime, and enhance productivity.

Security, scalability, and reliability remain key challenges for IoT growth, all of which hinge on continuous advances in chip design. As the number of connected devices soars into the tens of billions, microchips will form the invisible nervous system of a truly interconnected world.

Chapter 8

The Global Microchip Industry

Beneath the surface of every digital innovation lies a sophisticated and often invisible network of chipmakers, designers, and logistical powerhouses. The global microchip industry is one of the most complex and essential value chains in the modern world, touching everything from smartphones to satellites. It's also a battleground for economic power and geopolitical influence, with countries racing to secure dominance over this critical technology.

While the average consumer rarely thinks about where their device's chips come from, the reality is that each microchip is the product of a vast, interconnected industry. It's a sector defined by collaboration and competition—between design houses and foundries, suppliers and manufacturers, nations and corporations. At its core is a push toward ever-smaller, faster, and more efficient chips, and the strategic advantage they bring.

Key Manufacturers and Industry Leaders

The semiconductor industry is dominated by a few giants whose names are synonymous with innovation and scale. These companies represent the backbone of modern electronics, investing billions into research, development, and fabrication.

Intel, long recognized as a pioneer in CPU technology, has been a key driver in personal computing and data center chip design. Though it once dominated manufacturing as well, it now faces fierce competition from newer players in cutting-edge fabrication.

Taiwan Semiconductor Manufacturing Company (TSMC) is the world's leading semiconductor foundry. TSMC produces chips for major brands like Apple, NVIDIA, and AMD, and is known for its advanced manufacturing capabilities, including leading-edge nodes as small as 3 nanometers. Its role is so vital that the global electronics industry depends on its uninterrupted operation.

Samsung Electronics, based in South Korea, is another major player in both memory and logic chips. With dual roles as both designer and manufacturer, Samsung competes at the highest levels of both innovation and output.

NVIDIA and AMD dominate the GPU market, but they do not manufacture their chips. Instead, they design them and rely on foundries like TSMC to bring them to life—a business model that has reshaped the industry's structure.

Broadcom, Qualcomm, and MediaTek are among the leaders in communications and mobile chips, powering everything from 5G phones to Wi-Fi routers.

These leaders form the keystones of a highly competitive yet interdependent landscape—each leveraging its strengths to supply the ever-growing demand for smarter, faster, and more connected devices.

Fabless Companies and Foundry Models

The industry's evolution has given rise to a defining shift: the separation between chip design and chip manufacturing. This is known as the fabless-foundry model, where companies focus exclusively on design, outsourcing the manufacturing to specialized fabrication facilities.

Fabless companies, like Qualcomm, NVIDIA, AMD, and Apple, pour resources into designing high-performance, low-power, and feature-rich chips. They rely on Electronic Design Automation (EDA) tools, IP licensing, and deep domain expertise to craft next-generation architectures.

Foundries, such as TSMC and GlobalFoundries, specialize in producing chips at scale. These facilities, known as fabs, are among the most advanced and expensive manufacturing sites in the world, requiring extreme cleanliness, precision tools, and enormous investment.

This division of labor allows for flexibility and specialization. Fabless companies can innovate faster without the burden of maintaining production facilities, while foundries focus on perfecting fabrication at the atomic scale.

Some companies, such as Intel and Samsung, operate under a vertically integrated model, designing and manufacturing their own chips. Intel has recently begun offering foundry services to external clients, signaling a shift toward a hybrid strategy.

The fabless-foundry relationship has enabled a global semiconductor ecosystem that's agile and efficient—but also vulnerable, as the pandemic and trade disputes have revealed.

Supply Chain Dynamics and Logistics

A single microchip's journey from design to delivery can span over 20 countries and dozens of suppliers. This intricate supply chain involves raw materials, fabrication, testing, packaging, and distribution—each requiring specialized skills and infrastructure.

Raw materials like silicon wafers, rare earth elements, and high-purity chemicals are sourced from around the globe. Companies like Shin-Etsu (Japan) and SUMCO (Japan) dominate wafer production, while others supply essential gases and metals.

Fabrication is typically done in countries with advanced fabs, such as Taiwan, South Korea, the United States, and increasingly, China. Each chip must pass through multiple photolithography stages, chemical processes, and ion implants—tasks that demand billion-dollar machinery and ultra-clean environments.

Packaging and testing occur in different locations, often in Southeast Asia, where labor is more affordable. Chips are encased in protective materials and tested for defects and performance.

Logistics play a critical role in shipping completed chips to manufacturers across the globe. Whether destined for a car, a smartphone, or a data center, chips must arrive on time, often just as assembly begins. Any disruption—be it from a natural disaster, pandemic, or political tension—can send shockwaves throughout the supply chain.

The complexity of the semiconductor supply chain makes it both a marvel and a vulnerability. Every link must function flawlessly to keep the digital world running.

The Chip Shortage and Its Global Consequences

In 2020, a perfect storm disrupted the semiconductor supply chain, triggering a global chip shortage that reverberated across industries. What began as a pandemic-induced production pause quickly spiraled into one of the most disruptive supply crises in recent history.

Demand for consumer electronics surged as remote work and virtual learning took hold, while automotive companies, anticipating a slowdown, canceled chip orders. When demand roared back, carmakers found themselves at the back of the line, unable to secure the chips needed for production.

Automakers were hit hardest, with assembly lines idled and vehicle shortages driving up prices. Smartphones, gaming consoles, medical devices, and even household appliances were affected. Some companies began redesigning products to use fewer or more available chips.

The shortage exposed the fragility of global dependencies. With so much production concentrated in Taiwan and South Korea, geopolitical tensions and natural disasters became significant threats. It also highlighted how just-in-time inventory models—while efficient in normal times—offered little buffer in crisis.

Governments and corporations began reassessing their strategies. Emergency stockpiles, increased investment in domestic fabs, and new supplier relationships became priorities. The shortage turned semiconductors into a household topic and a matter of national urgency.

Geopolitical Influence and Technological Sovereignty

Semiconductors are no longer just economic assets—they are strategic resources. As digital infrastructure and military systems increasingly rely on advanced chips, control over semiconductor technology has become a national security issue.

The U.S. and China are locked in a tech rivalry centered on chip access. The United States has restricted Chinese companies' access to advanced manufacturing tools and chip designs, citing security concerns. In response, China has accelerated its own semiconductor development efforts, investing billions in R&D and domestic capacity.

Other nations have joined the race for technological sovereignty. The European Union has launched the European Chips Act, aiming to double its share of global chip production. India, Japan, and others are also offering incentives to attract chipmakers and build local capacity.

Export controls, such as the U.S. restrictions on advanced lithography tools made by ASML in the Netherlands, have heightened tensions and reshaped supply networks. Companies must now navigate an environment where business decisions intersect with diplomatic strategy.

Semiconductors are the new oil—critical to economic power, innovation leadership, and national defense. As countries seek to reduce dependence on foreign fabs and secure their digital futures, the semiconductor industry will remain at the center of global policymaking and technological ambition.

Conclusion

In the grand story of human progress, certain inventions serve as inflection points—moments when the course of history pivots, unlocking possibilities once relegated to the realm of imagination. The microchip is one of those pivotal innovations. What began as an effort to reduce the size and complexity of electronic circuits has evolved into a force that redefined the 20th century and became the heartbeat of the 21st.

From humble beginnings in the laboratories of Bell Labs and Texas Instruments, the journey of the microchip has been one of relentless innovation, problem-solving, and transformation. The transistor, once the size of a fingernail, is now embedded by the billions onto chips no larger than a postage stamp. And these chips, though nearlyinvisible to the naked eye, exert a profound influence on modern civilization. They are the silent, indispensable engines behind a world increasingly defined by digital intelligence, instantaneous communication, and technological convergence. Microchips have transformed the way we work, communicate, heal, travel, and even understand the universe.

The microchip's evolution has paralleled—and enabled—the evolution of society itself. As they became smaller, faster, and more efficient, the devices that relied on them became more powerful and accessible. This democratization of technology gave rise to the information age, where knowledge is not bound by geography or privilege, and where innovation is no longer limited to vast corporations or research institutions.

Throughout this book, we've explored the anatomy of microchips, the manufacturing process, and the types that serve different purposes: CPUs that process data, GPUs that render complex graphics, memory chips that store and retrieve information, and microcontrollers that make everyday objects "smart." We've unpacked the specialized roles of ASICs, the flexibility of FPGAs, and the all-in-one integration of SoCs. These technologies, although complex in their engineering, are united by a common thread—they all extend the capabilities of humanity.

In daily life, the impact of microchips is often invisible but omnipresent. They operate within the devices we use without a second thought: smartphones that connect us, vehicles that drive smarter, wearable devices that monitor our health, and home systems that respond to our voices. In hospitals, microchips power life-saving machines and advanced diagnostic tools. In industries, they control robotic arms, ensure supply chain precision, and optimize logistics. In the financial world, they secure transactions, power encryption, and enable high-frequency trading.

The microchip's reach also extends into sectors that define the future. Artificial Intelligence, with its ability to learn, reason, and adapt, relies heavily on microchips designed specifically for AI workloads. The rise of quantum computing, although still experimental, hints at a future where microchips behave in ways that defy classical physics, opening new frontiers in science and security. Meanwhile, the growth of edge computing and 5G connectivity demands chips that are not only powerful but energy-efficient and scalable.

Yet for all its achievements, the microchip industry is not without its challenges. The global chip shortage that emerged during the COVID-19 pandemic exposed the fragility of global supply chains. The delayed production of goods, from consumer electronics to automobiles, showed how deeply reliant we are on semiconductors. It also sparked a geopolitical awakening—a realization that technological sovereignty is as critical as military or economic independence.

Nations began to reevaluate their strategic priorities, resulting in policy shifts and massive investments. The U.S. CHIPS and Science Act, the European Chips Act, and similar initiatives in China, South Korea, and Japan underscore a global race not just for innovation but for control over production, research, and development. At the heart of these moves lies a simple truth: microchips are not just tools—they are the infrastructure of national power in the digital era.

This urgency has sparked debates over globalization versus self-reliance, efficiency versus resilience, and innovation versus regulation. It's clear that the next phase of the semiconductor revolution will be shaped not only in labs and fabs but also in legislative halls and international diplomacy.

Another key dimension of the future is sustainability. The manufacturing of microchips is resource-intensive, requiring significant amounts of water, chemicals, and rare materials. As the demand for chips continues to soar, so too must the industry's commitment to environmentally responsible practices. From more efficient fabrication techniques to circular economy strategies that recycle and reuse components, the green transformation of semiconductor production is no longer optional—it is imperative.

Parallel to this is the need for ethical frameworks that govern the use of microchip-enabled technologies. As chips power surveillance systems, AI-driven decision-making, and autonomous weaponry, societies must grapple with the moral implications. Who is accountable for decisions made by machines? How can we prevent bias encoded in algorithms? What safeguards are needed to protect privacy and individual rights in a world dominated by data?

The answers will not come easily, but the questions must be asked—and urgently. As stewards of such powerful tools, we must be vigilant, transparent, and inclusive in our approach. The microchip may be a product of engineering, but its impact is deeply human.

Another vital piece of the puzzle is education. The world needs more engineers, scientists, and technologists who not only understand how to build microchips but how to apply them creatively and responsibly. Bridging the skills gap is essential for sustaining innovation, and that requires investment in STEM education, vocational training, and cross-disciplinary programs that integrate ethics, policy, and design.

Inclusivity, too, is essential. A diverse workforce fuels richer ideas and more robust problem-solving. Ensuring that people from all backgrounds have access to careers in microchip development is not only equitable—it's smart business. The challenges of the 21st century demand all hands on deck.

As we look ahead, several trends will define the next era of microchip innovation:

Heterogeneous Computing: Combining different types of processors (CPU, GPU, AI accelerators) on a single platform to optimize performance and power efficiency.

Neuromorphic Chips: Inspired by the human brain, these chips mimic neural networks and could transform fields like robotics and real-time pattern recognition.

Chiplets and Modular Design: Moving away from monolithic chip designs toward a modular architecture that allows different components to be developed independently and assembled efficiently.

Quantum Chips: Exploiting the principles of quantum mechanics to achieve computational feats that are impossible for classical chips.

AI-Driven Design: Using machine learning to accelerate chip design itself, creating feedback loops that continuously improve performance and reduce development cycles.

All of these trends suggest that the pace of innovation is not slowing—it's accelerating. But the human capacity to adapt, understand, and regulate this innovation will be just as critical as the technology itself.

In closing, the microchip tells a story not just of silicon and electrons, but of ambition, ingenuity, and possibility. It reflects the best of what we can achieve when we harness science to solve problems and improve lives. It also serves as a reminder that with great power comes great responsibility.

As we move into an increasingly connected, intelligent, and automated world, the microchip remains at the center of it all—a silent sentinel driving progress forward.

Let us honor its legacy by using it wisely, understanding it deeply, and innovating with purpose. The pulse of the digital age beats within it—and with each new generation, that beat grows stronger, faster, and more profound.

The future is not only digital—it is microchipped. And that future, powered by precision and driven by dreams, belongs to all of us.